Silent Violence with Petals

Silent Violence with Petals

Poems by

Charlotte Cosgrove

© 2022 Charlotte Cosgrove. All rights reserved.
This material may not be reproduced in any form, published,
reprinted, recorded, performed, broadcast,
rewritten or redistributed without
the explicit permission of Charlotte Cosgrove.
All such actions are strictly prohibited by law.

Cover design by Ian Ryan
Book cover layout by Shay Culligan

ISBN: 978-1-63980-151-0

Kelsay Books
502 South 1040 East, A-119
American Fork, Utah 84003
Kelsaybooks.com

For my son and daughter
William and Emily

With special thanks to Helen Gibbon for all her encouragement

Acknowledgments

The following poems were first published, either online or in print, by the following publications:

Northern Otter Press: "Expectant Mother"
Dreich: "Unoccupied"
Lothlorien Poetry Journal: "Sorry For Your Loss"
Trouvaille Review: "A Box We Don't Need"
Dreich: "Mould Chasing"
Dreich: "Snowing in April"
Dreich: "Hyacinths"
The Literary Yard: "Floating Shelves"
Dreich: "Charity Shop"
The Literary Yard: "Roman de la poire"
The Literary Yard: "Grief"
Lothlorien Poetry Journal: "Things With No Owners"
The Literary Yard: "The Waiting Generation"
Confingo: "Gutting Fish"
Wingless Dreamer Spring Anthology: "The Room at the Back of the Vets"
The Broadkill Review: "The Cold Catching Competition"
Dreich: "Death is a Cat"
Bindweed Magazine: "The Day's Events"
The Broadkill Review: "Epidural Legs"
The Literary Yard: "Your Time of Year"
New Contexts 2 Anthology—Cover Story Books: "Fantasy Addiction"
Beyond Words: "Flowers on a Lamppost"

Contents

Expectant Mother	13
Unoccupied	14
Sorry for your Loss	15
Icy Streets in which we see Ourselves	16
A Box We Don't Need	17
Compassion for the Undertaker	18
Mould Chasing	19
Snowing in April	20
Hyacinths	21
Dandelion Teeth	22
Spider	23
Rose Petals	24
Floating Shelves	25
Charity Shop	26
Roman de la poire	27
Grief	28
Gathering Evidence	29
How We Learn	30
Things With No Owners	31
The Waiting Generation	32
Gutting Fish	33
Lonely Journeys	34
Taking Cover	35
The Room at the Back of the Vets	36
The Cold Catching Competition	37
Death Is a Cat	38
The Day's Events	39
Epidural Legs	40
Birthday Card	41
Coats in July	42
Antique shop	43
Your Time of Year	44

Bringing Us Together	45
Saving it for Best	46
Seeing You Again	47
Fantasy Addiction	48
Passing	49
Coming Last	50
Flowers on a Lamppost	51

Expectant Mother

You walk towards me opening up your coat.
Touch it, you say.
Great big mass of belly.
It reminds me of children's stick-on night lights.
I want to press you, see if you glow.
You are a moon cut through the middle.
You've never been so assured.
Your hair is falling out, your feet are swollen.
They look like you have kicked a bee's nest.
None of that matters because you have realised
This child you carry is a time traveller.
It is nursing your dead grandmother's smile
And will laugh the way your aunt used to.
When you are gone it will carry you in its being,
As you are carrying it, in yours.

Unoccupied

February. Rain bled invisibly
From the sky.
Soaked in seconds,
Sweating from dreams.
It was a crystal ball that forebode—
Days in the garden, nights cuddled
Indoors. The radiators were long
Stretched accordions—
Click-clacking, musically, like engines.
A single sock was wedged down the back
Mummified in dust.
As we turned the corner
We watched it disappear.

Sorry for your Loss

They told me he was lost—

Like keys.
My mother trying to remember the last jangle
Before she placed them down.
Forgot where she put him.
I was angry she could be so careless.
I wasn't even allowed to take something to the shop
In case I lost it.

I started looking under beds for him,
Round the back of the shed,
The linen cupboard.

I wandered through the front door
Searching for him.
She would always find me—
Arms limp at my sides
Like broken stalks.

She guided me back indoors.
Apologised to family and friends
By telling them—
She's just so lost.

Icy Streets in which we see Ourselves

There's ice on the streets, mirrors
In which we watch ourselves.
We suspend our bodies in concentration—
To not fall.
For if we do—
We see the purest vision
Of ourselves, smashed
And bundled on the ice.

A Box We Don't Need

There is a box still filled with things.
For over a month it has been in the hallway.
Dust has gathered around its bottom corners.
It's settling in, cushioning itself.
Brown tape is beginning to lift at the sides.
Beginning to expose itself to hair, dust, and minuscule insects.
It is a trap.
Inviting us to open it.

Compassion for the Undertaker

His feet press gently on the pedals
More pianist than driver.
The black hearse slows to the church
An inkblot spreading on white paper.
He opens the door for the grieving
Remains solemn as duty expects.
His eyes look down at pebbly gravel
Feels it within him as if made of concrete or hard minerals
Ready to decompose into the ground.
It has been just a week since he returned
After his compassionate leave came to an end.

Mould Chasing

I am chasing mould in this house.
Not frantically, more predatorial.
I am taking my time,
Laying in wait.
Sometimes I think I have found some, but it's just old bits
Of dirt on the skirting board.
My mother taught me that cleaning skirting boards
Should be done whenever there is a free minute.
If I sit on the toilet and see dust forming
On the wood I must stop and wipe.
It will only harden, worsen,
Will take over the room before I'm aware.
When I moved in there were patches
Of mould on the ceiling—dark spirits
Without faces. We became experts in mould
With their gladiatorial sounding names—
Cladosporium, Fusarium, Aspergillus, Trichoderma.
Seemingly undefeatable.
I would stay awake and watch the different shapes forming,
Checking as more black dots appeared,
Like a teenager counting blackheads.
Some patches were symmetrical, beautiful even,
Rorschach's inkblot test decorating the walls.
When you got the problem sorted there was discomfort
As I waited for it to return.
Now I spend my days ready. To catch before it spreads.
I have pulled out the bed in search of dropped jewellery
And there it is—fluffy, moist,
Damaged.

Snowing in April

It's snowing in April.
Swathes of snow melt and vanish as quickly as they come.
Children search in bedroom drawers for gloves and hats and
Scarves that trail blunderingly down the stairs like wedding trains.

They roll magic white orbs from the ground.
Assemble fairy dust from car windscreens to throw
At moving targets.

I bend down, eager.
There are small stains in the snow
Of rust and soil—
Food colouring haemorrhaging in the snow
I try for the untouched patch,
I gather, I inspect—but stones appear.

Hyacinths

Veins grew in bunches on her legs.
She wore polyester skirts to the knee
With see through tan tights that held
And wrapped bouquets of hyacinths.
Her legs were crossed at the ankles, scissor-like.
I imagined touching them, and them,
Feeling like dried porridge oats.
Later on I inspect my own mother's legs
As she sits vacant.
They are not purple yet,
More like the beginnings of a lilac based watercolour.

Dandelion Teeth

Skinny yellow legs, uncountable,
Like too many teeth crossed over.
Wet the beds, wee the beds, piss the beds,
Weeds.
Dying, ghostly fluff in the wind.
They are nature's bubbles for children who
Pick them, give them as a gift.
And we put them aside, the garden's rejects.
Later on we pick them back up
Blow them away
Like a birthday wish,
Gone.

Spider

Sweeping hands like cherry pickers through webs—
Candy floss stuck to fingers.
The patterned craftsmanship depleted—
Unconsidered by unthinking hands.
Later a spider runs across the floor
Human limbs quicken on to furniture
Someone is called to dispose of it.
A scurrying away, an escaping of the slipper slap.
A few days pass—
He's an adventurer now,
A hitchhiker,
A nomad,
Nowhere left to be.

Rose Petals

There are rose petals floating on the bath.
They are dead fish rising to the top.
Reptilian in my hands as I sweep them up,
Leaving outlines,
Tattooed,
A skin on my water.
If I look I'm sure to find a box
Of chocolates,
A giant teddy bear wearing a red bow,
Limp,
His head lolled left-wards.
A card
With a verse I won't read.
Cheap.

Floating Shelves

The noughties arrived with magical wood on the walls.
I was dazzled.
A perfect straight line, a scar on the wall—
Still healing, raised.
Hidden hinges, magic architecture.
My parents bought one, erected it in their bedroom.
Three candles, spaced out—
Not daring to touch each other.
A synchronised backing band,
Sleeping on driftwood.
They had a spare, gave it to me.
Over time I tested it, tried to quantify its greatness.
Boxes were piled and filled
Up to the ceiling. From the bed I threw objects
Like basketballs towards them.
Eventually they poked out at different angles,
Peeking at me. Worms rising from the soil.
Until one day it lay fallen
Shapeshifting into a raised floorboard.
The boxes spewed their belongings
And it occurred to me, with a shiver,
I hadn't heard the thud.

Charity Shop

My father brings me things that my mother doesn't want.
They are all second hand, old pieces of tat.
I wonder why you bought most of them.
Some I like—decorative plates, miniature books,
an old milkmaid's stool.
Nobody wants these things anymore—
They are not *fashionable*.
I dot these things around my home like splashes
Of paint on a canvas.
My father has gone shopping today.
My mother has gone with him
To actively discourage him.

Roman de la poire

The first time the heart
came out of the body
As a token
It was cradled
In the hands of man
Gifting his affection
With a pear.
He must
Have been sweating
Longing for
The sumptuousness
Of the fruit.
For her to take
A bite.
Peel the skin
With her teeth
Spit it
Sideways.
Offer him back
His fruit
Naked, dribbling.
And him,
Unsure
How to take it.

Grief

It is far more unexpected than waves.
It lies dormant but alert.
It is the disc that is threatening to slip,
The anaesthetic that is about to wear off.
One simple movement that creates spasms.
It is a sepulchrum prism and you
Are woven deep inside—cavernous
You cannot see the light refracting outside.
You search for an exit,
Until you give up
And have to sit
In the midst of it all.

Gathering Evidence

You have forced me to remember
Every time you have left the house
And not returned within the hour.
Or gone to the shops
And come back with just a coke.
You have become migratory.
I am alert when you tell me—
Just going to see my mum.
When I leave for work on your day off
I wonder if you will stay solitary for those hours.
I smell the bed sheets and check the pillows
For hair when I return, for another being.
Then on Sunday we go for a drive
And I see it.
I am a magpie, drawn
To the shining metal in the footwell.
A hairclip.
I put my shoe on it, territorial
Of this new information—
A child who has just found a bank note
With no intention to share.
You go in the petrol station to pay
And buy me cheap coffee.
I pick it up, roll it between my fingers,
Tasteful, delicate.
I call my friend but she tells me,
You need more.

How We Learn

She used to create her own newsletters
And give them out on the side of the road.
These words were loved and nurtured.
At first people took them, thanked her,
And without looking directly at her,
Smiled at the girl who willed change
To smash into her like a meteor.
They folded them neatly once or twice,
Put them in their pockets for later.
After a while nobody bothered to pretend
That they would read them.
They would ignore her, or worse,
Take one and screw it up—
Drop the rough white moon at her feet
Until she was standing like Saturn between them all.
Nobody remembered her face.
She was a mask clad wraith
Who they wished they had read.

Things With No Owners

A book of stamps, one peeled away
Like part of a satsuma.
I wonder if she knew
That the stamps would outlive her.
It could have been anything,
The twenty pence piece that had slipped through
The bag's shoddy lining.
Did a shiver run down her spine
As the shop girl handed it to her
Crumpled in the receipt.
A modest shining gift,
Dropped in the bag.
Falling into the unsewn cavity.
Lost objects.
Things with no owners.

The Waiting Generation

I imagine my parents when I was a child
Going to visit someone and not having a clue
If they were going to be in. Jumping
On buses and trains, walking
To far places in the hope that somebody
Would answer. Pilgrimaging to shops
On Sundays, unsure of the opening times.
Standing outside waiting for 11am.
Booking Spanish holidays off the teletext.
No phones or internet. Research meant
Going to the library. Talking
On landlines with cords
Unfurling and cascading on shoulders
Like a descending spiral staircase.
You all waited for taxis to turn up
At a rank. The sex of your babies—
A surprise. Programmes circled
In the TV guide for later.
Your children wait for nothing.
They want it all
And they want it now.

Gutting Fish

You were gutting a fish when I told you
I knew.
You hunched, bloody, over the worktop
In my apron.
Some sort of Jack-of-all-trades
Butcher Baker.
You must have realised
Instantly.
You ceased slicing,
Placed down your tools
Without sound in slow motion—
I can play it back.
So many times I had told you not to bring
Dead things home.
It wasn't enough that you killed it,
You took it apart,
Cut it straight through the middle.

Lonely Journeys

Next to their name is always green, available.
A mass,
An object,
Something in the way
When walking through lonely crowds.
Tables full of other people's friends
Their eyes never drift over.
Always the same faces on the train
Every morning.
One of them has noticed she hasn't seen them for a while.
She puts her earphones in, lifts her head
Smiles at the people walking past.
They move, like druids, looking down at their feet.

Taking Cover

Stabilising wetness.
The sound clogs up space in my mind.
Its theatrical—
With an interlude.
Black clouds,
Capes in the sky,
Open like curtains.
People scatter into doorways—
Cockroaches in colour.
Rubbing their hands together masterfully
As if it is aeons ago
And they are the fire makers.

The Room at the Back of the Vets

Thanks
I said to the Vet
After he'd killed the cat.
Black fluff like an old blanket
Lay on cold metal.
We went home, made coffee,
Cried.
We had no idea what happened when we left.
Did he take off his rubber gloves
And never think about it again?
Did he bundle you up into his arms
And throw you into a bin
Like one of those they have in the supermarket car park?
I wonder if there's a stray hair
Somewhere stuck between the grooves
That the cleaner will wipe away
In the morning—
Without realising.
And you'll be gone,
Completely.

The Cold Catching Competition

I did not *catch* this cold.
You didn't hurl it towards me like a rugby ball,
Arms reflexive as it thundered closer.
We lay in bed two nights ago, you fell asleep
First. I heard the soft pop of your mouth
Like beer opening.
Your breathing quietly roared for hours.
It saw me. Spirited its way over—
Wraith-like. Caressed my ears, nose and
Throat. When the morning comes
We share the burden—
Flaming heads, dithering feet.

Death Is a Cat

Her body is alive with death.
It rampages delicately through
Organs, blood, veins.
By daybreak it will quit.
Grow colder and revert
Into someone else, somewhere else.
It will move along the corridor and meow
Outside doors to come in.
Not thinking, or caring, or knowing
Whose door it sits at.
It will jump onto any bed, curl up
And stay awhile.

The Day's Events

I have a knack for seeing these things before they occur.
I am not bragging, There's no third eye or
Sixth sense. I just watch, listen,
Replay. Every conversation, meeting,
I am actively eavesdropping.
I have played it over, become surveillance.
As if I sit in an office chair, spinning, a long black
Cylinder shooting down from the seat
Splaying out in four legs, an animatronic
Praying mantis. Multiple screens play,
Like bathroom tiles but with moving pictures
Entitled: *The Day's Events*.
Because of this constant monitoring I am tired when I see you two
Together, the looks, the ease, the sudden
Disinterest in your respective partners.
And I wonder if you already know
How this will play out. Or, if I'll have to wait
For the footage to be played.

Epidural Legs

Sometimes I try to recreate feelings—
Play director to myself.
I lay down as straight as I can on the bed and pretend
I can't move my legs.

From the waist down there's nothing
Just two dead trunks in front of me
Like painted white pipes.

I remember two women came in and gave me
What I can only describe as a bed bath.

They hoisted me upwards,
Lifted one leg
At a time,
One arm
At a time.
Wiped the sweat from my face,
The blood from my body.
I, a life sized doll.

Someone came in with toast—
Slices as thick as bricks,
With butter that dripped on my dirty nightdress.

And now as I am recalling all this
I have given myself a cramp. And nobody
Will rub it better because it was too long ago
When it was my time.

Birthday Card

I'm reading an old birthday card from you.
I hadn't realised how much of you there still was—
In boxes, shelves, backs of cupboards.
You have written in black but it's barely there.
Ink that hardly touches the page.
The envelope is licked, sealed.
You probably left it on the mantelpiece
For when you next saw me.
Did you know there was something wrong?
Was it just another off day?
Because it was someone else
Who handed me the card.

Coats in July

A whole family in red and yellow mackintoshes,
Pieces in a boardgame, peppers on salad.
It's as if they don't sweat, they are boiling
Frogs in water.
They could be from somewhere warmer where
Our hot is their cold.
Maybe the parents are
Forcing the children to wear their coats.
Keep that coat zipped up, you'll catch your death.
The sky begins to blacken,
Dirty bath water.
Hail assails—earthbound,
Burning my skin with gravitational disregard,
As unapologetic as arrogance.
The family lift their hoods over their heads,
Pulling the drawstrings—
They are faces—
Encased in plastic shells.

Antique shop

The antique shop holds things from when we were children.

Matchbox toys and gaudy staring ornaments—
Clowns blowing trumpets with dripping white porcelain
Gathering dust in glass cabinets.

Do you remember these?
My brother holds up a set of crocheted doilies
Just like our grandparents used to have.
I don't tell him that I have them
Secreted at the bottom of an ottoman
Nurturing old ornaments like shrouds,
Just in case they are due
A comeback.

Your Time of Year

It is the way the light hits the floor that stops me.
Unblinkingly lighting the wood.
I can hear the birds outside—magpies
That just won't shut up. And it dawns on me
That this is the time of year,
The time of day that is you.
You would still go to the park
At this time. 3pm at the end of May.
Everyone else was packing up to leave,
But you knew that at this time
The birds would be louder, insects
Less hidden. And as I see this
Chink of light on the floorboard
I think you are with them now,
Somewhere in the air.

Bringing Us Together

Waves become still and solid
As I breathe them in.
I heave as they hit the back of my throat,
A mighty punch of earth in my larynx
Salting my insides in preservation—

We are here.
I can see you as my breath
Is gifted back to me like wrapped eternity.
You bob violently up and down—

Flotsam and jetsam in ecstasy.
You lean backwards baptismally—levitating.
I follow as the current splinters our skin,
Lacerations and punctures on us like rubber wheels.
I hope the current will smash us into each other
As if we are broken plates, discarded objects.

Saving it for Best

There is no saving it for best.
Programmes you wait until the weekend to watch,
Clothes you save for occasions—
Daughters want to wear ball gowns for bed,
Watch their favourite film for a five minute interval—
They've got it right,
There is no best.
There is now.
There is me, stopping
To watch the children play
As I unpeg the washing.

Seeing You Again

When I saw you again I hadn't expected
How old you would look.
Lines lay around your eyes,
Your mouth sat in the middle of tender slashes.
There was newness to them as if
I could peel them away like old stickers.
You couldn't tell I was shocked, you were just happy.
You stood on the pavement—part of it,
Slabs sat together with dried concrete reflecting
The foundation on your face, polyfillering
Cracks in plaster.

Fantasy Addiction

I have an addiction to fantasy.
I am a celebrity dating another celebrity.
That man coming out of the shop is my long lost father.
I have won an Oscar, a Pulitzer, a Grammy
And my personal favourite: a Nobel Prize
For absolutely anything.
I have won Miss World with my glowing complexion,
My supple chest and proclamation of world peace.
All this whilst simultaneously opening and running
A homeless shelter, single-handedly.
I am the detective in the movie who always cracks the case,
The best singer in the whole musical,
The millionaire with the good heart.
And like all good fantasies I try to cling on
Too hard, so tight it crushes—
Tiny pieces of different lives all over the floor.
And it is my job to sweep them all up,
Try to piece the remnants together.

Passing

He's passed on, they told me.
I felt I should have known what this meant.
I thought maybe it was French—*pas 'ton*.
Some sort of all together word but punctuated.
I imagined Olympic torch bearers
Passing their torches from one to the other
Proud, sweaty, pointless.
I didn't get it.
And I was quite shocked when I realised

He'd just stopped.

Coming Last

Somebody has to be last to lose—
Their virginity,
Get married,
Raise a child.

There has to be—
Last at PE
Last to go home at the end of the night.

Somebody has to be last, to lose.

Flowers on a Lamppost

The petals are trampled
Loose, like old people skin
It happens again, endlessly
The quick reminder of life.
The world zooms by at 60 miles an hour
With its windows shut and radios turned up high
Oh turn it up I like this one.
Look at that over there.
Silent violence with petals.

About the Author

Charlotte Cosgrove is a Poet and English Lecturer from Liverpool, England. She has BA and MA degrees in English and Writing from Liverpool John Moores University. She is published in numerous print and online magazines and anthologies. Charlotte was recently shortlisted for the Julian Lennon poetry prize and has been shortlisted for the Loft Books poetry prize and short story prize. Charlotte is also the editor of *Rough Diamond Poetry Journal.*

www.ingramcontent.com/pod-product-compliance
Lightning Source LLC
Chambersburg PA
CBHW031206160426
43193CB00008B/531